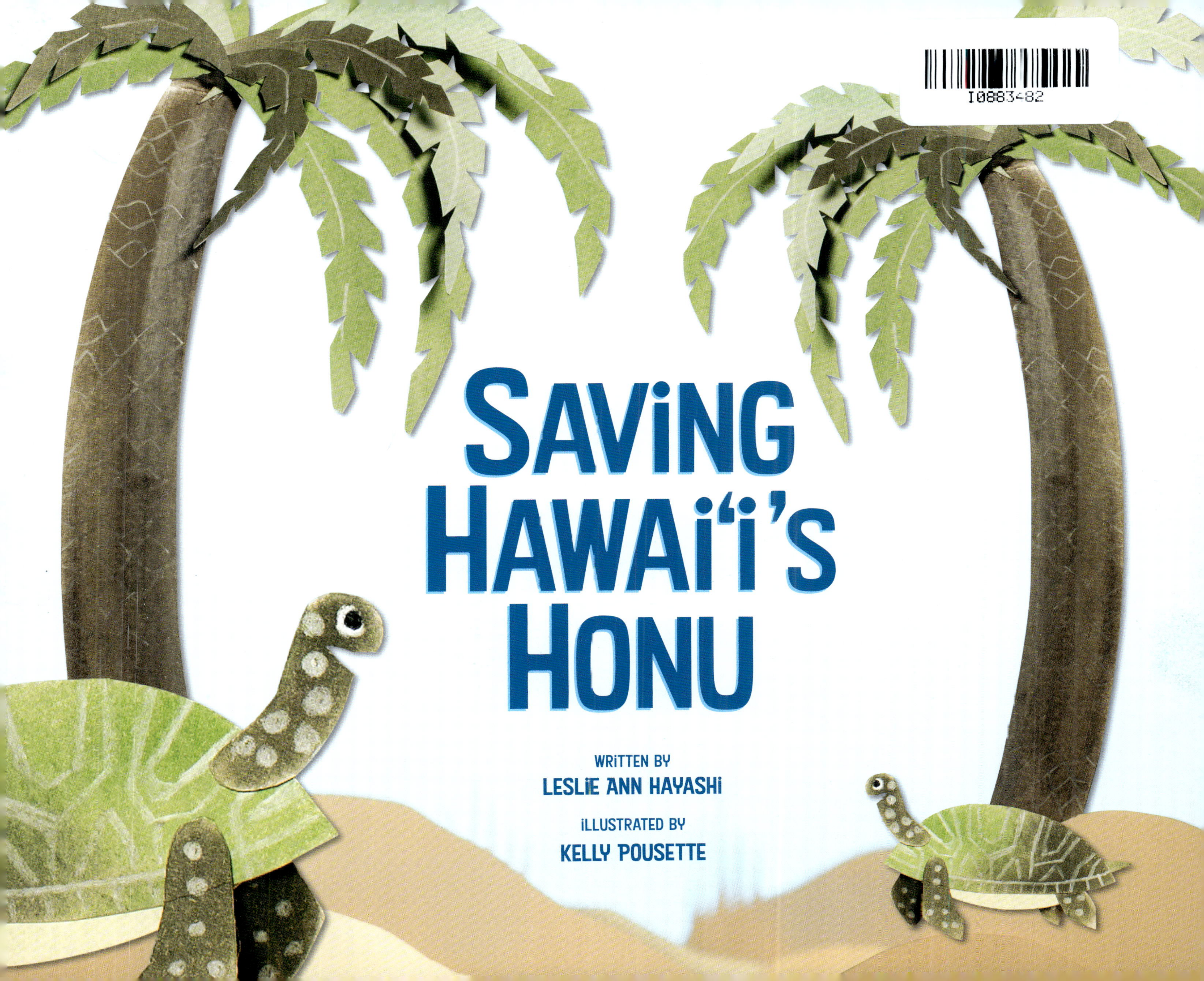

SAVING HAWAI'I'S HONU

WRITTEN BY

LESLIE ANN HAYASHI

ILLUSTRATED BY

KELLY POUSETTE

This book uses the okina, a Hawaiian diacritical mark, to accurately represent the pronunciation of Hawai'i in the Hawaiian language.

Reycraft Books
145 Huguenot Street
New Rochelle, NY 10801

reycraftbooks.com

Reycraft Books is a trade imprint and trademark of Newmark Learning LLC.

Library of Congress Control Number: 2024948716

Hardcover ISBN: 978-1-4788-6851-4
Paperback ISBN: 978-1-4788-7928-2

Photo Credits: Page 37D: AFP/Stringer/Getty Images;
Page 40: Newspix/Getty Images; All other images from Getty Images
Author photo: Courtesy of Dwight K. Okumoto
Illustrator photo: Courtesy of Dan Pousette

Printed in Dongguan, China. 8557/0225/22170
10 9 8 7 6 5 4 3 2 1

First Edition published by Reycraft Books 2025.

Reycraft Books and Newmark Learning LLC support diversity and the First Amendment, and celebrate the right to read.

REYCRAFT BOOKS

Mahalo nui loa to
George and the entire community
for their perseverance in bringing back
the honu from the brink of extinction.

And to my childhood friend,
Kathy Wong Bishop, for her idea to honor George.

George Balazs has never met a sea turtle he didn't like. And he's met hundreds... thousands... maybe hundreds of thousands of turtles.

He loves them all.

The funny thing is that he didn't even know what a sea turtle was when he was growing up in Yucca Valley, California.

There he only saw desert tortoises.

But his whole world changed while sailing in Tahiti as a young man.

That's when George saw his first honu,
or green sea turtle.

George then moved to Hawaiʻi and began studying animal science.

One day he noticed fishermen tossing live sea turtles into a large truck. He watched as the driver stopped at various restaurants and unloaded the turtles. In nearby stores, George also saw jewelry made from sea turtle shells.

Turtle steaks... turtle soup... turtle jewelry... That's when George asked the question that started his life's journey:

How many sea turtles are in Hawaiʻi?

Restaurant
TURTLE JEWELRY
SPECIAL turtle soup & steak

He asked his friends and fellow scientists.

"Don't worry," they told him.
"There are thousands of sea turtles."

But George wasn't convinced.

As a budding scientist, George knew there was only one way to answer his question.

He would have to count the turtles himself.

So George made plans to travel to the sea turtles' breeding grounds. The trip could be dangerous. For months, George would live on isolated beaches hundreds of miles away from home. He would have only the food and water he could bring with him.

When he arrived, George was greeted by the squawks and smells of nesting sooty terns.

If he got too close to their nests,
they attacked.

Immediately, George set up camp away from the terns and began tagging turtles in the darkness of night.

In time, George got used to the terns.

Beneath starry skies, George watched female turtles haul themselves onto the beach to lay their golf ball-sized eggs.

Using their large front flippers, they threw sand to cover their nests. Much of the sand ended up on their backs.

Slowly, the females returned to the sea,
never knowing if their eggs hatched.

At the end of the season, George stared at his notes. There were not thousands of turtles. Or even hundreds of turtles.

There were only...

...67 female turtles.

Unless people stopped killing them RIGHT AWAY, the turtles would be gone—extinct like the dinosaurs.

Once he returned home, George contacted reporters, legislators, anybody he could reach.

But no one would listen.

N

George wrote stories explaining that female turtles didn't lay eggs until they were at least twenty years old. Nor did they lay eggs every year. And only one in a thousand might get to age twenty.

George gave speeches, wrote more stories—anything to get the word out.

Finally, one day a newspaper published his story.

Honolulu Star-Bulletin

Then other readers shared their stories—of how the numbers of turtles were dwindling, of how high-powered spearguns were used to hunt them.

Soon the public took up George's cry to save the turtles. People volunteered to safeguard turtle eggs and release baby turtles into the ocean. They rescued injured and sick turtles.

Finally, laws were passed to protect the sea turtles.
It became a crime to kill a turtle or harm its nest.

Today, the honu are thriving once more.
Not just because George asked a simple question.

But because he had the courage to answer it.

TIMELINE TO TURTLE

1 **BEGINNING** Turtles mate.

2 **2 WEEKS LATER** Female lays eggs.

3 **2 MONTHS LATER** Eggs hatch and hatchlings head to sea; 90 percent are eaten by predators before they reach the ocean.

GROWTH

Once they become four to six years old, juveniles are the size of dinner plates. Their diet changes and they become herbivores, looking for tasty limu (seaweed) and seagrasses. A turtle's beak is shaped like a parrot's. While they have no teeth, their toothlike serrations allow them to snip and graze, earning them the nickname "lawn mowers of the sea."

When they are three to four years old and are approximately 20 or more inches long, they return to the beaches. In Hawai'i both males and females bask on the shore, which is unique.

Nesting females usually return to their birthplace. When the female lays its eggs, the sex of the turtles is not yet determined. Warmer sand temperatures produce females, while cooler ones produce males.

Honu can live up to sixty years in the wild.

1 in a 1000 will survive to adulthood

4 **4-6 YEARS LATER** They are young adults; sharks prey on many of them.

5 **20 OR MORE YEARS LATER** Females are able to mate.

HAWAIʻI'S GREEN SEA TURTLE FACTS

Honu are reptiles. Here are some facts about them.

A TURTLE'S SHELL

The shell is made up of two parts, the top carapace and the bottom plastron, which grow together around the turtle's body. A turtle can never leave its shell, just as we cannot leave our skin.

The carapace is darker in color, while the plastron is lighter, making it difficult for predators to spot the turtle from above and below.

Thin layers of keratin called scutes cover the turtle's shell. This same substance makes up people's fingernails.

FLIPPERS

A turtle's flippers are similar to a human's lower limbs. The upper parts of these "limbs" lie inside the turtle's shell. Unlike a tortoise, a honu cannot retract its neck and limbs into its shell. Sometimes a honu is missing a front or rear flipper due to a bite from its most common natural predator—the tiger shark.

HEART

Like most reptiles, turtles have three-chambered hearts. (Humans have four-chambered hearts.) By slowing its heartbeat and filling its lungs with air, a turtle can remain underwater for hours and dive to depths over 100 feet. They can also glide through the water for short bursts at up to 20 miles per hour, faster than any human can swim or run.

EYES

A turtle's eyes are covered with a black transparent membrane which provides superb sight underwater. However, on land a turtle is myopic, or nearsighted.

TURTLE ETIQUETTE

Here's what you can do to help the honu.

1. Learn about the honu.
2. Keep your distance whether on land or in the sea—at least 6-10 feet away.
3. Don't block a turtle's path to the ocean.
4. Don't use harsh cleaners or pesticides on your lawn.
5. Never let helium balloons escape.
6. Pick up discarded plastic bottles and bags.
7. Keep oceans and beaches clean and free of cigarette butts, plastics, and other debris.

Leslie Ann Hayashi

is a retired judge and author of numerous books, including *A Fishy Alphabet in Hawai'i*, *Aloha 'Oe: The Song Heard Around the World*, *His Majesty's Goldfish*, and *Baby Dino's First Lu'au*. In addition to writing, Leslie enjoys creating art and spending time with her family. She is married to Alan Van Etten, an attorney, and they have two adult sons, Justin and Taylor. She also has fun watching her first grandchild, Tanni, grow and learn about the world.

Kelly Pousette

is an illustrator originally from the west coast of British Columbia. Primarily self-taught, she experiments with both traditional and nontraditional techniques, often incorporating mixed media. Using paper-cut pieces and building dioramas, Kelly creates magical, whimsical stories and scenes. Her images often incorporate woodland critters and dynamic characters. Kelly currently resides in northern British Columbia with her husband and their very large dog, Clovis. Their frequent outdoor adventures only help encourage Kelly's imagination.